LOU-LOU
BABY MIRACLE

ZARA IKRAM
Author/Illustrator

Balboa Press books may be ordered through booksellers or by contacting:

Balboa Press
A Division of Hay House
1663 Liberty Drive
Bloomington, IN 47403
www.balboapress.com
1 (877) 407-4847

Illustrations credit: Zara Ikram

ISBN: 978-1-9822-4177-3 (sc)
ISBN: 978-1-9822-4178-0 (e)

Print information available on the last page.

Balboa Press rev. date: 01/25/2020

BALBOA.PRESS
A DIVISION OF HAY HOUSE

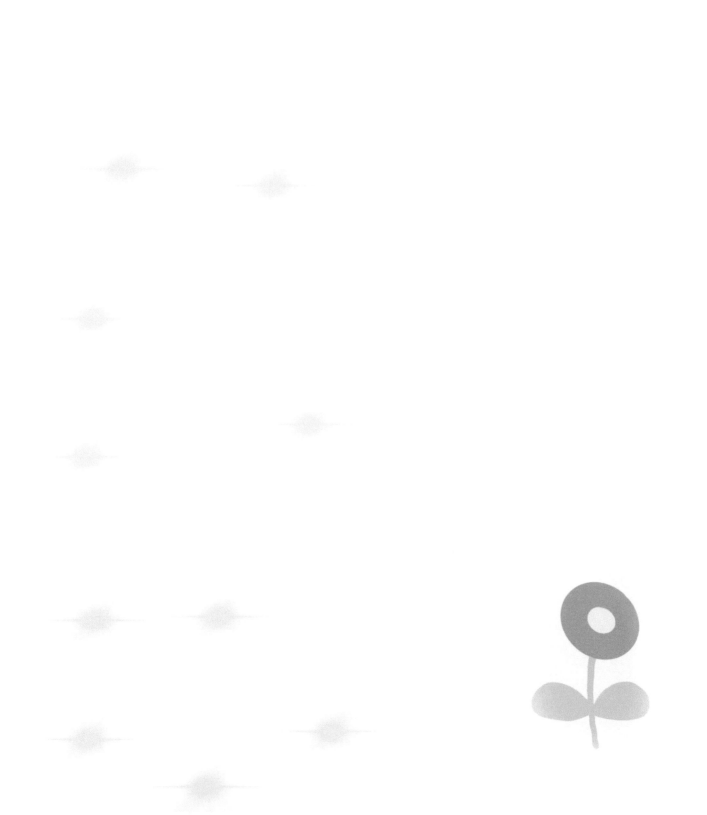

In a remote galaxy, among the universes
There lived a baby star light Lou-Lou

It went to school; it played and danced
It spread its joy with glitters.

It lived this way unknown term
As time is non-existent

In places outside of Earth
I know. It's weird, isn't?

A baby Lou-Lou lived this way
Until it sensed a new feeling
A yearning feeling for a place
It needed be for a reason.

Our star light baby went to school
And asked its wisest Teacher
"What is this tickling in my core
that I am elsewhere needed??"

The wisest Teacher paused in thought
Then kindly responded:

"It looks like time has come for you
To travel abroad. On a program".

"What is it? Tell me more!!
Please-please!!" exclaimed excited Lou-Lou.
"Well, it's a voyage to the Earth
For a human life experience."

"What is it "human"?
Please explain!" baby Lou-Lou was eager.

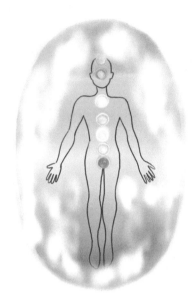

"Same light and energy like us
But looking somewhat different
They have a denser form than us
Their speaking – is also different.

They come in various shapes and forms
And colors and convictions
But all are equal at the core
There is no difference, really.

I know, I know – the Teacher laughed –
These new terms are too confusing

But you will learn them very fast"
Wise Teacher smiled convincingly.

"Wow!! All these sound so cool and new!
I want to travel! Really!
What do I do? Where do I go?"
Acted Lou-Lou too zealously.

"All right, all right – the Teacher said –
I see you are too eager
I'll take you to a place star lights
Pick their travel itineraries."

They walked together to a place –
A kind of a theater –

With big white screen and many seats
For baby start lights, typically.

Projector shed the light on screen
And pictures went in sequence
Narrator's Voice went all along
With stories for each screen piece.

In one, It showed two human forms
And called them "man" and "woman"
It said the two were "newlyweds"
In what's called "marriage union"
And now expecting a "newborn"
To join their brand new "family."

A call went on among star lights
Who'd like to choose this family
One star light raised its little hand
Wanting to go quite happily.

The Voice approved
and guided it next
To go to a travel office
To meet its tour
guides for a debrief
And get its travel
documents.

Next image slide came up on screen. On it two other humans
Who – Voice explained – were also
joined in a happy, loving union
Now these two men want to become parents for two siblings
Making arrangements for what it takes
to build their little family.

Two lookalike star lights jumped up
Exclaiming chance was theirs
Approved, proceeded to pick up
Their own travel itineraries.

A lot of other slides were shown
Of various coupled humans

All very different - yet One -
Love shining through these unions.

And just before next slide came up
Lou-Lou's heart went on beating
It pounded loud, very hard
It nearly skipped its beating.

Disturbed, Lou-Lou looked up on screen
And saw a human being
Who looked so beautiful in Light
And also too familiar..

Aaaahhh.....

Though by herself, she was complete
She was so whole and loving
The only heart's desire she had
Was to become a Mother.

Lou-Lou's heart pounded oh, so hard!
As if in a recognition
That a woman showing on the screen
Was someone very dear.

That yearning feeling? All that time?
Now had revealed its meaning!

"That's her! My Mom!!" Lou-Lou just screamed
And swirled in a happy dancing
Then pleaded to the Voice
"Please! Please! Allow me be her miracle!"

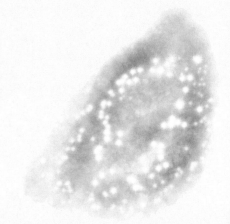

Approved, Lou-Lou ran to pick up
Its own travel itinerary.

A travel agent well described
The date and time of travel
And all details of a new life embraced in loving care
Of a woman waiting with all her might
For a beloved baby.

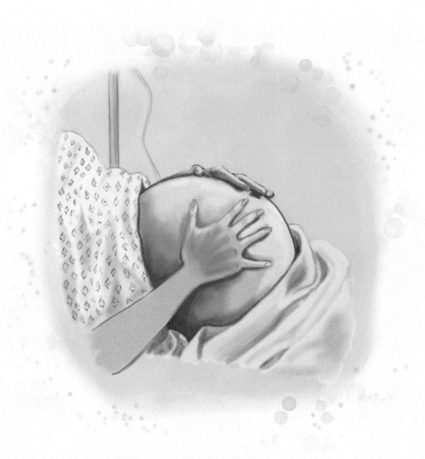

On that same day, as was defined,
Through a wormhole (Light Channel)

Lou-Lou swished to Mom's
womb and heart
And born was little Miracle!

About the Author

Corporate consultant by day, Zara Ikram (author's pen name) is an artist, children's books author and illustrator. Transformative life experiences have called Zara back to the life of art and creation in 2014. The latter were also catalytic to her founding of a nonprofit Pro-Cure Art (www.procure-art.org) that delivers healing arts and art therapy psychosocial support to people and communities affected by adversity. In awe with the divine intelligence of Life manifesting in all of creation, Zara aims to promote Its principles of love, harmony and beauty in her works of art and writing.

Printed in the United States
By Bookmasters